SERIESCRAFT 101:

SETTING AND WORLD-BUILDING WORKBOOK

PATRICIA GILLIAM

ISBN: 198567517X
ISBN-13: 978-1985675179

CONTENTS

INTRODUCTION

Like character creation, developing a believable fictional world is a process that becomes more defined with experience. If you're just starting out, however, planning your foundation will make the overall writing process a lot easier.

The initial idea of a story can come from almost anywhere, but creative elements of character, plot, theme, and setting all work together. It's often easiest to start in the area where you feel strongest. If an idea for a character feels solid to you, work backwards to figure out how the story's setting impacted your character. If you have a great plot idea first, make sure to balance it with a character who readers will remember and care about. Think about ways that setting can be used as a tool to deepen a character's development or move the story's plot.

Templates work well for characters and setting, but keep in mind that the majority of the information is for your personal reference as an author. Don't bombard your readers with a list of traits in the first few paragraphs. Readers don't like action interrupted, and too much description can bog down or interrupt the pacing of a story. Conveying physical environments through senses (not relying just on sight and sound) and showing cultural exchanges through action and dialogue are two approaches that work well.

According to your genre, some aspects of the following templates may be more useful than others. Don't feel obligated to fill in every segment prior to starting your story. As with characters, more ideas will develop while writing, and I've attempted to leave enough room for growth across multiple books.

Since different genres require different forms of settings, I've arranged the templates in this workbook by location and culture. If there's any aspect that is not applicable to your story, feel free to move on to the next segment.

Best wishes on your projects!

Patricia Gilliam

OVERVIEW QUESTIONS

1) What functions do you want setting to serve in the story?

2) Within your genre, what are some examples of great settings in books or movies? What aspects did you like about them?

3) What makes your fictional universe different from reality?

4) What is the scope of the locations across each book? Are you dealing with a range of several planets or a single home?

5) In a similar vein, how far into the past and future do you need to know outside of your main storyline?

6) If you're writing through a character's point-of-view, what aspects of the setting will be most important, interesting, or new?

SPECIFIC SETTING QUESTIONS & PROMTS

(USE WITH BLANK TEMPLATES IN LATER SECTIONS)

PART 1: PHYSICAL ASPECTS

PLANETARY-LEVEL DATA

*Gravity relative to Earth
*Atmosphere composition
*Rotation
*Orbit
*Placement near its sun
*Size
*Any moons? How many? What are their sizes?
*Closest planetary neighbors
*Polar regions
*Surface temperature range and variations
*Water availability
*Ability to support life (and what kinds)
*Potential hazards (frequent asteroid or comet impacts, etc.)
*How long could your characters survive if stranded?

GEOGRAPHY AND GEOLOGY

*If you're dealing with an actual location on Earth, print a map and mark key natural landmarks—mountains, rivers, lakes, canyons, etc. If you're creating a new location from scratch, researching multiple real-life locations can provide you a starting point.

*Think of the texture and amount of bounce to the soil. What are the color and make-up of it?

*Where are water sources? How are they used and/or filtered?

*Are there important mineral or fuel deposits nearby? If so, how are they mined or extracted?

*What natural resources are considered the most valuable in the area?

CLIMATE AND WEATHER

*What would the weather be on a typical day?

*What are the seasons like? How often do they change?

*What major weather events are predictable?

*What events could catch your characters off-guard?

WILD VEGETATION

*Different trees and plants need certain conditions to thrive. For example, evergreens tend to do well in wet temperate areas while cacti can survive areas with long dry spells.

*Wooded and rainforest areas tend to have multiple layers of plant life—ferns and shrubs more toward the ground-level, etc. What plants may a character brush up against while walking outside?

*Does the vegetation have an overall pleasant or unpleasant smell?

*In urban settings, are there still parks? Where are they located?

CULTIVATED VEGETATION

*Are there any fruits or vegetables grown locally?

*What kinds of flowers and trees are found near houses?

*Do characters have gardens?

*How are crops grown, harvested, preserved, and cooked?

WILDLIFE

*Main categories would include mammals, birds, reptiles, fish, amphibians, insects, and arachnids.

*Ecosystems similar to Earth will have a variety of herbivores (grazing animals), carnivores (hunters/scavengers), and omnivores (can eat plants or animals based on availability).

*Used biology textbooks and nature websites are great resources.

*With sci-fi and fantasy, consider starting with a real animal or set of animals for inspiration.

*Think in terms of how they would move and behave, what they eat, and what could be considered a threat.

*What makes them able to survive their environment?

*With populations and frequency of sightings, keep in mind that there are normally a lot more prey species than predators—and everything needs a source of food and water. (If something is out of balance, you may need to seed why—especially if it's important to the story.)

DOMESTICATED ANIMALS

*These can range from farm and labor animals (horses, oxen, cows, pigs, chickens, etc.) to pets.

*How they are treated can be a reflection of a culture.

*If a character had a wild animal as a pet, how would the situation be viewed by the overall society?

PART 2: CULTURAL ASPECTS

POPULATION AND COMMUNITY

*Think of this in broad terms of how the population's size will impact the daily life of your characters. For example, daily life in a large city will generally have a feel of urgency to it compared to a small town.

*How do people relate with each other? Is the community close-knit, or do people tend to keep to themselves whenever possible? Why?

*What are key parts of the community's identity? What holds it together? (Possible examples could be anything from a company or sports team to a major event that impacted the entire area.)

SOCIAL STRUCTURE

*Does the society have a class-system (official or non-official)?

*How easy is it to move in societal position?

*What personal traits or occupational positions are considered valuable in the society? Which ones are devalued or looked down upon?

*Are there different role expectations for men and women? What about adults and children?

RELIGION AND MORALITY

*What do people believe and value?

*What impact do spiritual matters have on moral behavior and other areas of society?

*How do people view life and death?

TRADITONS, MAJOR LIFE EVENTS, AND HOLIDAYS

*How are major life events treated?

*How are holidays celebrated?

*What are the differences in behavior and dress?

*Are there customs related to daily events?

FAMILY AND FRIENDSHIPS

*The atmosphere within a family home can be in contrast or a reflection of the outside world.

*How do the values of a character's family and close friends impact him or her?

*Think about how objects within a home can trigger past memories.

*The degree of order or messiness in a location can be a reflection of personality.

GOVERNMENT AND LAW

*What is the overall governmental structure of the society? How did it form?

*How are laws created and enforced?

*How prevalent is crime?

*What types of crime are common and uncommon?

POLITICS

*What are the levels (such as national, state, local) and structure?

*What sides are involved, and what does each believe?

*What are potential conflicts/topics in everyday conversations?

ECONOMY, COMMERCE, AND CURRENCY

*What is the economic system in place?

*What can be owned by individuals or groups? Is anything regulated or restricted? Why?

*What is considered currency? Are services or products ever bartered?

*Is the overall economy thriving or floundering in the background? What industries and companies are doing well? What industries are in decline? Why?

*Is poverty a severe problem or rare? What are the major methods of wealth building in the society?

*How might these aspects affect individual characters?

DAILY LIFE AND ROUTINE

*It's helpful to take a look at your own life as an example and apply this to your characters and setting.

*How is time treated and measured? Is it acceptable to be late or early to a meeting or event? Are work and rest periods on any particular days or cycles?

*What places and people are familiar to your character?

*Does your character tend to be at the same places on daily basis, or is there a variety to the week or month?

*Will these locations be important to the plot in some way?

*What forms of infrastructure do your characters encounter every day—plumbing, electricity, roads, garbage service, postal service, etc.?

*Keep in mind sensory details here—everything from the taste of toothpaste to the smell of the character's workplace.

OCCUPATIONS

*Certain job positions can have their own sub-culture with jargon the average person may not understand. You can sometimes still incorporate this by putting things within context so the reader can figure out what is meant.

*Pay careful attention with careers you're not familiar with on a personal basis—if possible, verify that you're accurate in the portrayal with an authority in that field.

TOOLS AND TECHNOLOGY

*Consider the technology characters will come across throughout their day, including forms of transportation and communication. How are vehicles and buildings made? What materials are used? Is there a recognizable design that would identify the manufacturer?

*What are the layouts of cities, commercial areas, homes, and forms of transportation? With smaller devices, what is the functional layout? (Sketches are great for this.)

*If you need full historical accuracy, make sure you don't have anything that didn't exist during your timeframe (an extreme example would be an iPod in the 1940s, but there are more subtle details that some readers will notice if you're sloppy).

*With futuristic technology, it's helpful to look at current on-the-horizon advancements and take them to a point where they're widely available to the public.

COMMUNICATIONS AND MEDIA

*How does general news spread?

*How are private messages sent? If more than one language is spoken or written, how is this addressed (technology, interpreters, etc.)?

*How long does it take for information to reach distant recipients?

*How are the media systems structured? Is there a variety in options or only one main source?

*What are some forms of entertainment media—movies, shows, music, etc.?

ARTS AND MUSIC

*What instruments are played? What is the history of music for your culture? Who are the major musicians? Apply the same questions to painters, writers, and other crafts.

*Art and music can also help establish timeframe—for example, songs from particular eras can be mentioned at strategic points to show a progression of time. (Be sure to research all applicable copyright laws and permissions regarding the use of actual lyrics.)

*Are there major locations dedicated to displays or performances? (Can show value and importance to that art.) What is their layout?

FASHION AND DRESS

*Clothing can be an indication of social status, occupation, and personality (including situations where dress is in conflict with what someone would typically expect)

*Do certain colors, textures, or styles mean anything?

*Overall trends can be used to indicate timeframe.

*What are the variations between casual and formal situations?

*What are common and rare forms of jewelry and accessories?

FOOD AND MEALS

*A large percentage of our sense of taste depends on smell, which is why foods don't taste quite the same when you have a cold, etc. Keep this in mind with sensory details.

*Meals can range from a required ritual to survive to an elaborate social event. When you have a meal in your story, consider the purpose behind it and how you can use it to reveal information about your characters.

*Are there any manners or traditions associated with meals?

*How are strangers/guests treated?

*Are certain foods/drinks rare or only for special events?

*Are there anything considered taboo to eat from a culture standpoint?

EDUCATION

*How are children taught? Are there formal schools or some other form of education? What is the age range for training?

*What would a typical day look like for a student?

*How is education viewed by the overall society? Are certain forms of education considered more valuable over others?

*Is continued learning important to the adult population?

WAR AND MILITARY

*If any, what peoples are at odds with each other and why? What groups are allies and are willing to defend each other?

*What methods does the society used to defend itself against attackers?

*When are militaries formed? How are they trained?

*What are the overall ranks, structures, and divisions of military forces? How are promotions handled?

*How are troops supplied and compensated?

*Are there any wars that have a historical impact on the setting?

*What forms of weapons and technology are used?

MEDICAL, HEALTH, AND ILLNESS

*What types of medical care are in place?   What is the degree of technological advancement?

*What are common illnesses? Are they season-related? What diseases are rare? What is and isn't curable?

*How is medicine viewed by the culture? What are the moral safeguards in place? What happens when and if someone crosses a line?

*What is the overall health and average lifespan of the population? Why?

LOCATION 1:_____

Location Type (Planet, City, Town, Home, etc.):

Map or Layout Sketch:

Overview Description:

Physical Geography, Geology, and Major Landmarks:

Climate and Weather:

Wild Vegetation:

Cultivated Vegetation:

Wildlife:

Domesticated Animals:

Population:

Social Structure:

Government and Law:

Politics:

Economy, Commerce, and Currency:

Traditions, Major Life Events, and Holidays:

Family and Friendships:

Daily Life and Routine:

Occupations:

Tools and Technology:

Communications and Media:

Arts and Music:

Fashion and Dress:

Food and Meals:

Education:

War and Military:

Medical, Health, and Illness:

Additional Notes and Sketches:

LOCATION 2:_____

Location Type (Planet, City, Town, Home, etc.):

Map or Layout Sketch:

Overview Description:

Physical Geography, Geology, and Major Landmarks:

Climate and Weather:

Wild Vegetation:

Cultivated Vegetation:

Wildlife:

Domesticated Animals:

Population:

Social Structure:

Government and Law:

Politics:

Economy, Commerce, and Currency:

Traditions, Major Life Events, and Holidays:

Family and Friendships:

Daily Life and Routine:

Occupations:

Tools and Technology:

Communications and Media:

Arts and Music:

Fashion and Dress:

Food and Meals:

Education:

War and Military:

Medical, Health, and Illness:

Additional Notes and Sketches:

LOCATION 3:_____

Location Type (Planet, City, Town, Home, etc.):

Map or Layout Sketch:

Overview Description:

Physical Geography, Geology, and Major Landmarks:

Climate and Weather:

Wild Vegetation:

Cultivated Vegetation:

Wildlife:

Domesticated Animals:

Population:

Social Structure:

Government and Law:

Politics:

Economy, Commerce, and Currency:

Traditions, Major Life Events, and Holidays:

Family and Friendships:

Daily Life and Routine:

Occupations:

Tools and Technology:

Communications and Media:

Arts and Music:

Fashion and Dress:

Food and Meals:

Education:

War and Military:

Medical, Health, and Illness:

Additional Notes and Sketches:

LOCATION 4:_____

Location Type (Planet, City, Town, Home, etc.):

Map or Layout Sketch:

Overview Description:

Physical Geography, Geology, and Major Landmarks:

Climate and Weather:

Wild Vegetation:

Cultivated Vegetation:

Wildlife:

Domesticated Animals:

Population:

Social Structure:

Government and Law:

Politics:

Economy, Commerce, and Currency:

Traditions, Major Life Events, and Holidays:

Family and Friendships:

Daily Life and Routine:

Occupations:

Tools and Technology:

Communications and Media:

Arts and Music:

Fashion and Dress:

Food and Meals:

Education:

War and Military:

Medical, Health, and Illness:

Additional Notes and Sketches:

LOCATION 5:_____

Location Type (Planet, City, Town, Home, etc.):

Map or Layout Sketch:

Overview Description:

Physical Geography, Geology, and Major Landmarks:

Climate and Weather:

Wild Vegetation:

Cultivated Vegetation:

Wildlife:

Domesticated Animals:

Population:

Social Structure:

Government and Law:

Politics:

Economy, Commerce, and Currency:

Traditions, Major Life Events, and Holidays:

Family and Friendships:

Daily Life and Routine:

Occupations:

Tools and Technology:

Communications and Media:

Arts and Music:

Fashion and Dress:

Food and Meals:

Education:

War and Military:

Medical, Health, and Illness:

Additional Notes and Sketches:

LOCATION 6:_____

Location Type (Planet, City, Town, Home, etc.):

Map or Layout Sketch:

Overview Description:

Physical Geography, Geology, and Major Landmarks:

Climate and Weather:

Wild Vegetation:

Cultivated Vegetation:

Wildlife:

Domesticated Animals:

Population:

Social Structure:

Government and Law:

Politics:

Economy, Commerce, and Currency:

Traditions, Major Life Events, and Holidays:

Family and Friendships:

Daily Life and Routine:

Occupations:

Tools and Technology:

Communications and Media:

Arts and Music:

Fashion and Dress:

Food and Meals:

Education:

War and Military:

Medical, Health, and Illness:

Additional Notes and Sketches:

LOCATION 7:_____

Location Type (Planet, City, Town, Home, etc.):

Map or Layout Sketch:

Overview Description:

Physical Geography, Geology, and Major Landmarks:

Climate and Weather:

Wild Vegetation:

Cultivated Vegetation:

Wildlife:

Domesticated Animals:

Population:

Social Structure:

Government and Law:

Politics:

Economy, Commerce, and Currency:

Traditions, Major Life Events, and Holidays:

Family and Friendships:

Daily Life and Routine:

Occupations:

Tools and Technology:

Communications and Media:

Arts and Music:

Fashion and Dress:

Food and Meals:

Education:

War and Military:

Medical, Health, and Illness:

Additional Notes and Sketches:

LOCATION 8:_____

Location Type (Planet, City, Town, Home, etc.):

Map or Layout Sketch:

Overview Description:

Physical Geography, Geology, and Major Landmarks:

Climate and Weather:

Wild Vegetation:

Cultivated Vegetation:

Wildlife:

Domesticated Animals:

Population:

Social Structure:

Government and Law:

Politics:

Economy, Commerce, and Currency:

Traditions, Major Life Events, and Holidays:

Family and Friendships:

Daily Life and Routine:

Occupations:

Tools and Technology:

Communications and Media:

Arts and Music:

Fashion and Dress:

Food and Meals:

Education:

War and Military:

Medical, Health, and Illness:

Additional Notes and Sketches:

LOCATION 9:_____

Location Type (Planet, City, Town, Home, etc.):

Map or Layout Sketch:

Overview Description:

Physical Geography, Geology, and Major Landmarks:

Climate and Weather:

Wild Vegetation:

Cultivated Vegetation:

Wildlife:

Domesticated Animals:

Population:

Social Structure:

Government and Law:

Politics:

Economy, Commerce, and Currency:

Traditions, Major Life Events, and Holidays:

Family and Friendships:

Daily Life and Routine:

Occupations:

Tools and Technology:

Communications and Media:

Arts and Music:

Fashion and Dress:

Food and Meals:

Education:

War and Military:

Medical, Health, and Illness:

Additional Notes and Sketches:

LOCATION 10:_____

Location Type (Planet, City, Town, Home, etc.):

Map or Layout Sketch:

Overview Description:

Physical Geography, Geology, and Major Landmarks:

Climate and Weather:

Wild Vegetation:

Cultivated Vegetation:

Wildlife:

Domesticated Animals:

Population:

Social Structure:

Government and Law:

Politics:

Economy, Commerce, and Currency:

Traditions, Major Life Events, and Holidays:

Family and Friendships:

Daily Life and Routine:

Occupations:

Tools and Technology:

Communications and Media:

Arts and Music:

Fashion and Dress:

Food and Meals:

Education:

War and Military:

Medical, Health, and Illness:

Additional Notes and Sketches:

LOCATION 11:_____

Location Type (Planet, City, Town, Home, etc.):

Map or Layout Sketch:

Overview Description:

Physical Geography, Geology, and Major Landmarks:

Climate and Weather:

Wild Vegetation:

Cultivated Vegetation:

Wildlife:

Domesticated Animals:

Population:

Social Structure:

Government and Law:

Politics:

Economy, Commerce, and Currency:

Traditions, Major Life Events, and Holidays:

Family and Friendships:

Daily Life and Routine:

Occupations:

Tools and Technology:

Communications and Media:

Arts and Music:

Fashion and Dress:

Food and Meals:

Education:

War and Military:

Medical, Health, and Illness:

Additional Notes and Sketches:

LOCATION 12:_____

Location Type (Planet, City, Town, Home, etc.):

Map or Layout Sketch:

Overview Description:

Physical Geography, Geology, and Major Landmarks:

Climate and Weather:

Wild Vegetation:

Cultivated Vegetation:

Wildlife:

Domesticated Animals:

Population:

Social Structure:

Government and Law:

Politics:

Economy, Commerce, and Currency:

Traditions, Major Life Events, and Holidays:

Family and Friendships:

Daily Life and Routine:

Occupations:

Tools and Technology:

Communications and Media:

Arts and Music:

Fashion and Dress:

Food and Meals:

Education:

War and Military:

Medical, Health, and Illness:

Additional Notes and Sketches:

LOCATION 13:_____

Location Type (Planet, City, Town, Home, etc.):

Map or Layout Sketch:

Overview Description:

Physical Geography, Geology, and Major Landmarks:

Climate and Weather:

Wild Vegetation:

Cultivated Vegetation:

Wildlife:

Domesticated Animals:

Population:

Social Structure:

Government and Law:

Politics:

Economy, Commerce, and Currency:

Traditions, Major Life Events, and Holidays:

Family and Friendships:

Daily Life and Routine:

Occupations:

Tools and Technology:

Communications and Media:

Arts and Music:

Fashion and Dress:

Food and Meals:

Education:

War and Military:

Medical, Health, and Illness:

Additional Notes and Sketches:

LOCATION 14:_____

Location Type (Planet, City, Town, Home, etc.):

Map or Layout Sketch:

Overview Description:

Physical Geography, Geology, and Major Landmarks:

Climate and Weather:

Wild Vegetation:

Cultivated Vegetation:

Wildlife:

Domesticated Animals:

Population:

Social Structure:

Government and Law:

Politics:

Economy, Commerce, and Currency:

Traditions, Major Life Events, and Holidays:

Family and Friendships:

Daily Life and Routine:

Occupations:

Tools and Technology:

Communications and Media:

Arts and Music:

Fashion and Dress:

Food and Meals:

Education:

War and Military:

Medical, Health, and Illness:

Additional Notes and Sketches:

LOCATION 15:_____

Location Type (Planet, City, Town, Home, etc.):

Map or Layout Sketch:

Overview Description:

Physical Geography, Geology, and Major Landmarks:

Climate and Weather:

Wild Vegetation:

Cultivated Vegetation:

Wildlife:

Domesticated Animals:

Population:

Social Structure:

Government and Law:

Politics:

Economy, Commerce, and Currency:

Traditions, Major Life Events, and Holidays:

Family and Friendships:

Daily Life and Routine:

Occupations:

Tools and Technology:

Communications and Media:

Arts and Music:

Fashion and Dress:

Food and Meals:

Education:

War and Military:

Medical, Health, and Illness:

Additional Notes and Sketches:

LOCATION 16:_____

Location Type (Planet, City, Town, Home, etc.):

Map or Layout Sketch:

Overview Description:

Physical Geography, Geology, and Major Landmarks:

Climate and Weather:

Wild Vegetation:

Cultivated Vegetation:

Wildlife:

Domesticated Animals:

Population:

Social Structure:

Government and Law:

Politics:

Economy, Commerce, and Currency:

Traditions, Major Life Events, and Holidays:

Family and Friendships:

Daily Life and Routine:

Occupations:

Tools and Technology:

Communications and Media:

Arts and Music:

Fashion and Dress:

Food and Meals:

Education:

War and Military:

Medical, Health, and Illness:

Additional Notes and Sketches:

LOCATION 17:_____

Location Type (Planet, City, Town, Home, etc.):

Map or Layout Sketch:

Overview Description:

Physical Geography, Geology, and Major Landmarks:

Climate and Weather:

Wild Vegetation:

Cultivated Vegetation:

Wildlife:

Domesticated Animals:

Population:

Social Structure:

Government and Law:

Politics:

Economy, Commerce, and Currency:

Traditions, Major Life Events, and Holidays:

Family and Friendships:

Daily Life and Routine:

Occupations:

Tools and Technology:

Communications and Media:

Arts and Music:

Fashion and Dress:

Food and Meals:

Education:

War and Military:

Medical, Health, and Illness:

Additional Notes and Sketches:

LOCATION 18:_____

Location Type (Planet, City, Town, Home, etc.):

Map or Layout Sketch:

Overview Description:

Physical Geography, Geology, and Major Landmarks:

Climate and Weather:

Wild Vegetation:

Cultivated Vegetation:

Wildlife:

Domesticated Animals:

Population:

Social Structure:

Government and Law:

Politics:

Economy, Commerce, and Currency:

Traditions, Major Life Events, and Holidays:

Family and Friendships:

Daily Life and Routine:

Occupations:

Tools and Technology:

Communications and Media:

Arts and Music:

Fashion and Dress:

Food and Meals:

Education:

War and Military:

Medical, Health, and Illness:

Additional Notes and Sketches:

LOCATION 19:_____

Location Type (Planet, City, Town, Home, etc.):

Map or Layout Sketch:

Overview Description:

Physical Geography, Geology, and Major Landmarks:

Climate and Weather:

Wild Vegetation:

Cultivated Vegetation:

Wildlife:

Domesticated Animals:

Population:

Social Structure:

Government and Law:

Politics:

Economy, Commerce, and Currency:

Traditions, Major Life Events, and Holidays:

Family and Friendships:

Daily Life and Routine:

Occupations:

Tools and Technology:

Communications and Media:

Arts and Music:

Fashion and Dress:

Food and Meals:

Education:

War and Military:

Medical, Health, and Illness:

Additional Notes and Sketches:

LOCATION 20:_____

Location Type (Planet, City, Town, Home, etc.):

Map or Layout Sketch:

Overview Description:

Physical Geography, Geology, and Major Landmarks:

Climate and Weather:

Wild Vegetation:

Cultivated Vegetation:

Wildlife:

Domesticated Animals:

Population:

Social Structure:

Government and Law:

Politics:

Economy, Commerce, and Currency:

Traditions, Major Life Events, and Holidays:

Family and Friendships:

Daily Life and Routine:

Occupations:

Tools and Technology:

Communications and Media:

Arts and Music:

Fashion and Dress:

Food and Meals:

Education:

War and Military:

Medical, Health, and Illness:

Additional Notes and Sketches:

GROUP TEMPLATES

(USED FOR FAMILIES, ORGANIZATIONS, AND COMPANIES)

GROUP 1:_____

Group Type (Family, Organization, Company, etc.):

Members and Their Positions/Roles:

Overview History:

Importance to Story:

Interactions/Connections to Other Groups and Characters:

Motivations/What does the group want to achieve as a whole? (Individuals within the group may be in alignment or in conflict with these goals—or have differences on how to achieve them.)

Does the group have any symbols or logos to identify them?

What is the group's reputation (accurate or not)?

Additional notes and sketches:

GROUP 2:_____

Group Type (Family, Organization, Company, etc.):

Members and Their Positions/Roles:

Overview History:

Importance to Story:

Interactions/Connections to Other Groups and Characters:

Motivations/What does the group want to achieve as a whole?
(Individuals within the group may be in alignment or in conflict with
these goals—or have differences on how to achieve them.)

Does the group have any symbols or logos to identify them?

What is the group's reputation (accurate or not)?

Additional notes and sketches:

GROUP 3:_____

Group Type (Family, Organization, Company, etc.):

Members and Their Positions/Roles:

Overview History:

Importance to Story:

Interactions/Connections to Other Groups and Characters:

Motivations/What does the group want to achieve as a whole? (Individuals within the group may be in alignment or in conflict with these goals—or have differences on how to achieve them.)

Does the group have any symbols or logos to identify them?

What is the group's reputation (accurate or not)?

Additional notes and sketches:

GROUP 4:_____

Group Type (Family, Organization, Company, etc.):

Members and Their Positions/Roles:

Overview History:

Importance to Story:

Interactions/Connections to Other Groups and Characters:

Motivations/What does the group want to achieve as a whole? (Individuals within the group may be in alignment or in conflict with these goals—or have differences on how to achieve them.)

Does the group have any symbols or logos to identify them?

What is the group's reputation (accurate or not)?

Additional notes and sketches:

GROUP 5:_____

Group Type (Family, Organization, Company, etc.):

Members and Their Positions/Roles:

Overview History:

Importance to Story:

Interactions/Connections to Other Groups and Characters:

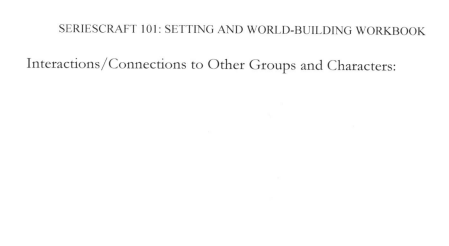

Motivations/What does the group want to achieve as a whole? (Individuals within the group may be in alignment or in conflict with these goals—or have differences on how to achieve them.)

Does the group have any symbols or logos to identify them?

What is the group's reputation (accurate or not)?

Additional notes and sketches:

GROUP 6:_____

Group Type (Family, Organization, Company, etc.):

Members and Their Positions/Roles:

Overview History:

Importance to Story:

Interactions/Connections to Other Groups and Characters:

Motivations/What does the group want to achieve as a whole? (Individuals within the group may be in alignment or in conflict with these goals—or have differences on how to achieve them.)

Does the group have any symbols or logos to identify them?

What is the group's reputation (accurate or not)?

Additional notes and sketches:

GROUP 7:_____

Group Type (Family, Organization, Company, etc.):

Members and Their Positions/Roles:

Overview History:

Importance to Story:

Interactions/Connections to Other Groups and Characters:

Motivations/What does the group want to achieve as a whole?
(Individuals within the group may be in alignment or in conflict with
these goals—or have differences on how to achieve them.)

Does the group have any symbols or logos to identify them?

What is the group's reputation (accurate or not)?

Additional notes and sketches:

GROUP 8:_____

Group Type (Family, Organization, Company, etc.):

Members and Their Positions/Roles:

Overview History:

Importance to Story:

Interactions/Connections to Other Groups and Characters:

Motivations/What does the group want to achieve as a whole? (Individuals within the group may be in alignment or in conflict with these goals—or have differences on how to achieve them.)

Does the group have any symbols or logos to identify them?

What is the group's reputation (accurate or not)?

Additional notes and sketches:

GROUP 9:_____

Group Type (Family, Organization, Company, etc.):

Members and Their Positions/Roles:

Overview History:

Importance to Story:

Interactions/Connections to Other Groups and Characters:

Motivations/What does the group want to achieve as a whole? (Individuals within the group may be in alignment or in conflict with these goals—or have differences on how to achieve them.)

Does the group have any symbols or logos to identify them?

What is the group's reputation (accurate or not)?

Additional notes and sketches:

GROUP 10:_____

Group Type (Family, Organization, Company, etc.):

Members and Their Positions/Roles:

Overview History:

Importance to Story:

Interactions/Connections to Other Groups and Characters:

Motivations/What does the group want to achieve as a whole? (Individuals within the group may be in alignment or in conflict with these goals—or have differences on how to achieve them.)

Does the group have any symbols or logos to identify them?

What is the group's reputation (accurate or not)?

Additional notes and sketches:

SERIES GLOSSARY

(TERMS UNIQUE TO THE UNIVERSE)

*Term:_____

Definition:

Origin:

Ways to provide context:

*Term:_____

Definition:

Origin:

Ways to provide context:

*Term:_____

Definition:

Origin:

Ways to provide context:

*Term:_____

Definition:

Origin:

Ways to provide context:

*Term:_____

Definition:

Origin:

Ways to provide context:

*Term:_____

Definition:

Origin:

Ways to provide context:

*Term:_____

Definition:

Origin:

Ways to provide context:

*Term:_____

Definition:

Origin:

Ways to provide context:

*Term:_____

Definition:

Origin:

Ways to provide context:

*Term:_____

Definition:

Origin:

Ways to provide context:

*Term:_____

Definition:

Origin:

Ways to provide context:

*Term:_____

Definition:

Origin:

Ways to provide context:

*Term:_____

Definition:

Origin:

Ways to provide context:

*Term:_____

Definition:

Origin:

Ways to provide context:

*Term:_____

Definition:

Origin:

Ways to provide context:

*Term:_____

Definition:

Origin:

Ways to provide context:

*Term:_____

Definition:

Origin:

Ways to provide context:

*Term:_____

Definition:

Origin:

Ways to provide context:

*Term:_____

Definition:

Origin:

Ways to provide context:

*Term:_____

Definition:

Origin:

Ways to provide context:

*Term:_____

Definition:

Origin:

Ways to provide context:

*Term:_____

Definition:

Origin:

Ways to provide context:

*Term:_____

Definition:

Origin:

Ways to provide context:

*Term:_____

Definition:

Origin:

Ways to provide context:

*Term:_____

Definition:

Origin:

Ways to provide context:

*Term:_____

Definition:

Origin:

Ways to provide context:

*Term:_____

Definition:

Origin:

Ways to provide context:

*Term:_____

Definition:

Origin:

Ways to provide context:

*Term:_____

Definition:

Origin:

Ways to provide context:

*Term:_____

Definition:

Origin:

Ways to provide context:

*Term:_____

Definition:

Origin:

Ways to provide context:

*Term:_____

Definition:

Origin:

Ways to provide context:

*Term:_____

Definition:

Origin:

Ways to provide context:

*Term:_____

Definition:

Origin:

Ways to provide context:

*Term:_____

Definition:

Origin:

Ways to provide context:

*Term:_____

Definition:

Origin:

Ways to provide context:

*Term:_____

Definition:

Origin:

Ways to provide context:

*Term:_____

Definition:

Origin:

Ways to provide context:

*Term:_____

Definition:

Origin:

Ways to provide context:

*Term:_____

Definition:

Origin:

Ways to provide context:

*Term:_____

Definition:

Origin:

Ways to provide context:

*Term:_____

Definition:

Origin:

Ways to provide context:

*Term:_____

Definition:

Origin:

Ways to provide context:

*Term:_____

Definition:

Origin:

Ways to provide context:

*Term:_____

Definition:

Origin:

Ways to provide context:

*Term:_____

Definition:

Origin:

Ways to provide context:

*Term:_____

Definition:

Origin:

Ways to provide context:

*Term:_____

Definition:

Origin:

Ways to provide context:

*Term:_____

Definition:

Origin:

Ways to provide context:

*Term:_____

Definition:

Origin:

Ways to provide context:

*Term:_____

Definition:

Origin:

Ways to provide context:

*Term:_____

Definition:

Origin:

Ways to provide context:

*Term:_____

Definition:

Origin:

Ways to provide context:

*Term:_____

Definition:

Origin:

Ways to provide context:

*Term:_____

Definition:

Origin:

Ways to provide context:

*Term:_____

Definition:

Origin:

Ways to provide context:

*Term:_____

Definition:

Origin:

Ways to provide context:

*Term:_____

Definition:

Origin:

Ways to provide context:

*Term:_____

Definition:

Origin:

Ways to provide context:

*Term:_____

Definition:

Origin:

Ways to provide context:

*Term:_____

Definition:

Origin:

Ways to provide context:

*Term:_____

Definition:

Origin:

Ways to provide context:

*Term:_____

Definition:

Origin:

Ways to provide context:

*Term:_____

Definition:

Origin:

Ways to provide context:

*Term:_____

Definition:

Origin:

Ways to provide context:

*Term:_____

Definition:

Origin:

Ways to provide context:

*Term:_____

Definition:

Origin:

Ways to provide context:

*Term:_____

Definition:

Origin:

Ways to provide context:

*Term:_____

Definition:

Origin:

Ways to provide context:

*Term:_____

Definition:

Origin:

Ways to provide context:

*Term:_____

Definition:

Origin:

Ways to provide context:

*Term:_____

Definition:

Origin:

Ways to provide context:

TIMELINE & HISTORY

*Can include events relevant to your main characters along with background events that shaped their cultures.

Major Event:_____

Date:

Location(s):

Key Character(s) Involved:

Event Details:

Major Event:_____

Date:

Location(s):

Key Character(s) Involved:

Event Details:

Major Event:_____

Date:

Location(s):

Key Character(s) Involved:

Event Details:

Major Event:_____

Date:

Location(s):

Key Character(s) Involved:

Event Details:

Major Event:_____

Date:

Location(s):

Key Character(s) Involved:

Event Details:

Major Event:_____

Date:

Location(s):

Key Character(s) Involved:

Event Details:

Major Event:_____

Date:

Location(s):

Key Character(s) Involved:

Event Details:

Major Event:_____

Date:

Location(s):

Key Character(s) Involved:

Event Details:

Major Event:_____

Date:

Location(s):

Key Character(s) Involved:

Event Details:

Major Event:_____

Date:

Location(s):

Key Character(s) Involved:

Event Details:

Major Event:_____

Date:

Location(s):

Key Character(s) Involved:

Event Details:

Major Event:_____

Date:

Location(s):

Key Character(s) Involved:

Event Details:

Major Event:_____

Date:

Location(s):

Key Character(s) Involved:

Event Details:

Major Event:_____

Date:

Location(s):

Key Character(s) Involved:

Event Details:

Major Event:_____

Date:

Location(s):

Key Character(s) Involved:

Event Details:

Major Event:_____

Date:

Location(s):

Key Character(s) Involved:

Event Details:

Major Event:_____

Date:

Location(s):

Key Character(s) Involved:

Event Details:

Major Event:_____

Date:

Location(s):

Key Character(s) Involved:

Event Details:

Major Event:_____

Date:

Location(s):

Key Character(s) Involved:

Event Details:

Major Event:_____

Date:

Location(s):

Key Character(s) Involved:

Event Details:

Major Event:_____

Date:

Location(s):

Key Character(s) Involved:

Event Details:

Major Event:_____

Date:

Location(s):

Key Character(s) Involved:

Event Details:

Major Event:_____

Date:

Location(s):

Key Character(s) Involved:

Event Details:

Major Event:_____

Date:

Location(s):

Key Character(s) Involved:

Event Details:

Major Event:_____

Date:

Location(s):

Key Character(s) Involved:

Event Details:

Major Event:_____

Date:

Location(s):

Key Character(s) Involved:

Event Details:

Major Event:_____

Date:

Location(s):

Key Character(s) Involved:

Event Details:

Major Event:_____

Date:

Location(s):

Key Character(s) Involved:

Event Details:

Major Event:_____

Date:

Location(s):

Key Character(s) Involved:

Event Details:

Major Event:_____

Date:

Location(s):

Key Character(s) Involved:

Event Details:

Major Event:_____

Date:

Location(s):

Key Character(s) Involved:

Event Details:

Major Event:_____

Date:

Location(s):

Key Character(s) Involved:

Event Details:

Major Event:_____

Date:

Location(s):

Key Character(s) Involved:

Event Details:

Major Event:_____

Date:

Location(s):

Key Character(s) Involved:

Event Details:

Major Event:_____

Date:

Location(s):

Key Character(s) Involved:

Event Details:

Major Event:_____

Date:

Location(s):

Key Character(s) Involved:

Event Details:

Major Event:_____

Date:

Location(s):

Key Character(s) Involved:

Event Details:

Major Event:_____

Date:

Location(s):

Key Character(s) Involved:

Event Details:

Major Event:_____

Date:

Location(s):

Key Character(s) Involved:

Event Details:

Major Event:_____

Date:

Location(s):

Key Character(s) Involved:

Event Details:

SPACE FOR FAMILY TREES AND TIMELINE SKETCHES

SPACE FOR FAMILY TREES AND TIMELINE SKETCHES

SPACE FOR FAMILY TREES AND TIMELINE SKETCHES

SPACE FOR FAMILY TREES AND TIMELINE SKETCHES

SPACE FOR FAMILY TREES AND TIMELINE SKETCHES

SPACE FOR FAMILY TREES AND TIMELINE SKETCHES

CONTINUITY & SERIES RULES

*These are concepts about the setting and characters that you want to keep consistent.

*You can adapt this to your genre. For example, fantasy authors can use this section for magic system information. Sci-fi authors can use it for space travel rules and technology limits. With superheroes and villains, you need to know the range limits and weaknesses of powers and abilities.

*Even if you never plan to bring in co-writers, imagine if the scope of the project required it. What would another writer need to know to write in your universe?

Rule:

First appearance in story:

Why it's important:

Additional details:

Rule:

First appearance in story:

Why it's important:

Additional details:

Rule:

First appearance in story:

Why it's important:

Additional details:

Rule:

First appearance in story:

Why it's important:

Additional details:

Rule:

First appearance in story:

Why it's important:

Additional details:

Rule:

First appearance in story:

Why it's important:

Additional details:

Rule:

First appearance in story:

Why it's important:

Additional details:

Rule:

First appearance in story:

Why it's important:

Additional details:

Rule:

First appearance in story:

Why it's important:

Additional details:

Rule:

First appearance in story:

Why it's important:

Additional details:

Rule:

First appearance in story:

Why it's important:

Additional details:

Rule:

First appearance in story:

Why it's important:

Additional details:

Rule:

First appearance in story:

Why it's important:

Additional details:

Rule:

First appearance in story:

Why it's important:

Additional details:

Rule:

First appearance in story:

Why it's important:

Additional details:

Rule:

First appearance in story:

Why it's important:

Additional details:

Rule:

First appearance in story:

Why it's important:

Additional details:

Rule:

First appearance in story:

Why it's important:

Additional details:

Rule:

First appearance in story:

Why it's important:

Additional details:

Rule:

First appearance in story:

Why it's important:

Additional details:

Rule:

First appearance in story:

Why it's important:

Additional details:

Rule:

First appearance in story:

Why it's important:

Additional details:

Rule:

First appearance in story:

Why it's important:

Additional details:

Rule:

First appearance in story:

Why it's important:

Additional details:

Rule:

First appearance in story:

Why it's important:

Additional details:

Rule:

First appearance in story:

Why it's important:

Additional details:

Rule:

First appearance in story:

Why it's important:

Additional details:

Rule:

First appearance in story:

Why it's important:

Additional details:

Rule:

First appearance in story:

Why it's important:

Additional details:

Rule:

First appearance in story:

Why it's important:

Additional details:

*For characters who are new to your world, what could get them into trouble or put them in danger without their awareness? What characters or groups would be there to help? Who would take advantage of the situation?

*What locations in your setting are considered "safe" for your characters? Which ones are dangerous? Think about ways you can convey either mood through the surroundings. (In some stories, an antagonist later breaks the perceived safety of a location during the story—or conversely, your protagonists may risk entering a territory you've established as hostile.)

*What aspects of everyday life (transportation, utilities, communication, cultural routines, etc.) can be disrupted? Think about this in terms of what characters value and deem important. What could delay their arrival to a major event or cause stress/tension?

*What problems and conflicts does your setting generate? What would make sense to add as part your plot?

SENSE OF WONDER

*What are the positive aspects of your setting that you want to highlight? What groups are either trying to solve problems and/or protect people?

*Are there locations that generate a sense of awe from the perspective of the characters?

*Small specific moments and actions have the potential to carry great emotional impact. What are potential opportunities for this within your setting?

ABOUT THE AUTHOR

Patricia Gilliam is the author of *The Hannaria Series* and Thaw (Kindle Worlds Novella). She is also a short story contributor to The Immortality Chronicles (*The Future Chronicles* series) and It's a Bird! It's a Plane! (Superheroes and Vile Villains). She and her husband Cory live in Knoxville, TN.

www.patriciagilliam.com

Made in the USA
Monee, IL
06 November 2021